Jennie Robinson

Germany's international aid programmes: her contribution to the different UN aid programmes

GRIN Verlag

Bibliografische Information der Deutschen Nationalbibliothek:

Die Deutsche Bibliothek verzeichnet diese Publikation in der Deutschen National-
bibliografie; detaillierte bibliografische Daten sind im Internet über http://dnb.d-
nb.de/ abrufbar.

Impressum:

Copyright © 2006 GRIN Verlag GmbH
Druck und Bindung: Books on Demand GmbH, Norderstedt Germany
ISBN: 978-3-640-40728-6

Dieses Buch bei GRIN:

http://www.grin.com/de/e-book/130410/germany-s-international-aid-programmes-
her-contribution-to-the-different

University of Malta

Department of International Relations

Course IRL 3090 Foreign Policy of Germany

Group Assignment – Presentation:

"Germany's international aid programmes:
her contribution to the different UN aid programmes"

Part 1 – Germany's aid policy and the UN

Jennie Hery-Jaona

B.A. (Hons.) 2nd year

Presented on April 6th, 2006

Introduction

Following the Second World War and in the context of the Cold War, reconstruction in Europe has led to the beginning of aid programme under American sponsorship. About a decade later, the European colonies, in the wake of independence and the years onwards, were the ones in need for aid mainly due to the gap in economic development leading to their poverty. Interests would still be the overriding aim for the donor to provide loans and other forms of assistance to the recipient countries. Also taking into consideration some advantages for the donors, international organizations such as the United Nations (UN) would become important means via which the funds would be transferred. Within this framework, this paper addresses German aid policy and its role in the UN.

Development

1.0 Some definitions

First of all there is a need to define several key terms which are going to be used throughout this paper. The definition of the following concepts derived from J. White[1]:

- 'Foreign aid': actions taken by people or institutions in one country towards people or institutions in another country which help, or are at least intended to help, the latter
- 'Aid': resources transferred between nations
- 'Development': the endeavours that aid supported
- 'Underdeveloped/developing/less developed countries/Third World': countries in which the institutions that received the resources were located

1.1 The recipient's perspective of aid

In the wake of independence, several factors led to developing countries' demand for aid. According to Clifford and Little these were: the fall in the prices of commodity from 1952, the running out of their external reserves by 1958, the cessation of grant aid due to independence, the different expenditures brought along with the phase of independence (e.g. overseas representation, new buildings for government and parliament, compensation for expatriates), and "the growing demands for demands for a better material standard of living".[2]

---

[1] White J., The Politics of Foreign Aid, pp.7-11
[2] Clifford J. M. & Little I.M.D, International aid, p.18

1.2 The donor's perspective of aid

On the other side, from the donor's perspective carrying out aid implied some national interests in return. For instance, "commercial motives have been strong; Germany, Italy, and Japan, began in the 1950s to compete for new markets, and export credit (frequently confused with aid) has been a major weapon".[3] Commercial interests still somehow depends on humanitarian concerns, i.e. "the whole benefit of aid to the donors arises via the enrichment of the recipient"[4]. Then, the interest in economic development is also taken into account since, "the primary self-interest of the Western powers lies in promoting the kind of régime which will be both viable and as non-aggressive and favourable to Western ideas as possible, and that reasonably egalitarian economic development is a means to do this".[5] However despite the involvement of bargain in aid, in the end the recipient was the one to abide to the obligations. The political or strategic factor was also to be considered not only during the Cold War scenario, but also with the argument that "development possibilities in a country depend very much on the political situation".[6]

1.3 Germany's aid policy

Germany's international aid programme is carried out within the context of German development policy, which was to become an independent aspect of German foreign policy. According to Perroy, Germany's aid doctrine has been set in terms of economic efficiency with the economic survival as the aim. Public funds were the means and aid was undertaken in the form of technical assistance from the Länder, industrials and private organizations. Private investments were seen to benefit both investors and host countries.[7] For Germany undertaking capital aid programme in the 1960s, meant also that "Germany as a legally re-established and respected state, was once again able to take its place in the world and to assume wide international responsibilities".[8] Indeed, the ideological context of the Cold War also influenced the promotion of "private enterprise in developing countries" since aid was considered to be "an essential political and commercial tool for any important power". Hence, "it was inevitable that Germany should become a donor on a substantial scale".[9] Germany's aid contribution or

---

[3] ibid., p.20
[4] ibid., p.79
[5] ibid., p.90
[6] Clifford J. M. & Little I.M.D, op.cit., p.85
[7] Perroy H., L'Europe dans le tiers-monde, pp. 105-109
[8] Perroy H., op.cit.,p.42
[9] ibid., p.43

capital inflow was mainly in the form of: financial, commodity aid, and technical assistance.[10] Aid policy laid on the principle that "aid should promote indigenous private enterprise" so that financial aid was to be used on projects, especially "for revenue-earning projects at commercial rates of interest, or for infrastructure investment at subsidized rates of interest".[11] By 1980, Germany was therefore to become the third largest DAC (Development Assistance Committee) contributor after the USA and France, with 13% of ODA (Overseas Development Assistance).[12]

German development policy however evolved since the 1950s. By the 1970s it needed to be redefined and the following principles were to be considered:[13]

- improvement of the financial conditions for aid measures (easier credit, more technical help on a grant basis)
- minimal tying of loans to procurements from West Germany
- upgrading the multilateral provision of loans via international organizations
- co-operation with a series of partner countries to be carried out on a long-term basis which were to take the form of comprehensive country programming

In the year 1980, following the Report of the Independent Commission on International Development Issues chaired by Willy Brandt (known as the Brandt Commission), the Development Policy Guidelines included these issues[14]:

- giving priority to combating extreme poverty
- rural development (in particular to guarantee the provision of food)
- the use of conventional and non-exhaustible energy sources
- the protection of natural resources

In 1986, the coalition of Democrats and Liberals considered the following points[15]:

- development can only take place through the mobilization of the "creative energy of the people in the countries concerned"
- the necessary framework for "help towards self-help" must be established by the developing countries themselves
- without formally imposing the principles of a market economy, recipient countries with a free market orientation and an open social system should be given priority

---

[10] ibid., p.159
[11] ibid., p.43
[12] Selim H., Development assistance policies and the performance of aid agencies, p.97
[13] Malek M.H., Contemporary issues in European development aid, pp.45-46
[14] ibid., p.48
[15] ibid., p.49

- whenever deliveries from industrialized countries are necessary in order to sustain or set up projects, they should come primarily from West German suppliers
- education and training, which should not follow inappropriate Western models and curricula
- the role of women in the development process, which must be considered more clearly
- support in the field of structural adjustment, which is to gain more importance

By 1988, Germany, with its ODA amounting at $4.7 billion, ranked fourth among the largest aid donors, after the USA, Japan and France.[16]

1.4 Criteria for foreign aid

With regard to the criteria to be taken into consideration for foreign aid, the respective Ministry referred to[17]:

- the general economic and social situation
- the potential for foreign trade
- effects made by developing countries to help themselves
- the capacity for absorbing foreign capital
- population size
- political aspects

1.5 Increasing the budget for development cooperation

In 2005, Federal Ministry for Economic Co-operation and Development's (BMZ) budget is 76 million euros larger than last year, an increase of 2 percent. The Development Ministry is thus one of the few ministries that the German government wants to strengthen, also showing the importance German parliament gives to development cooperation.[18]

---

[16] Malek M.H., op.cit, p.51
[17] ibid., pp.55-56
[18] <http://www.bmz.de/en/figures/GermanContribution/index.html>

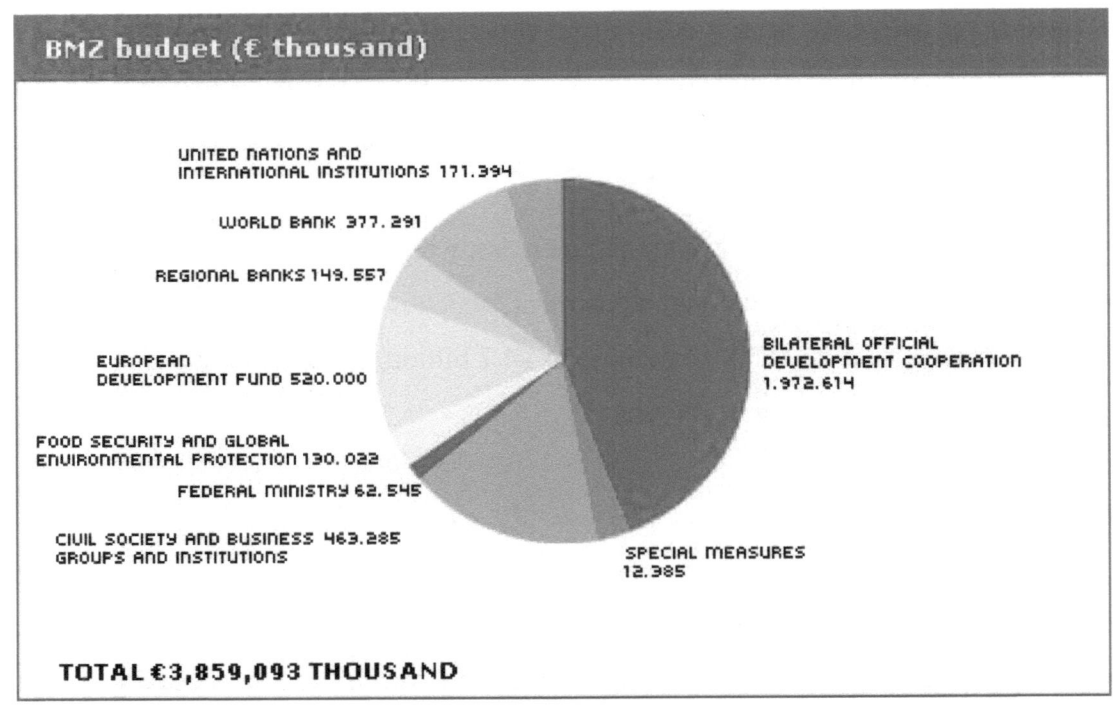

TOTAL €3,859,093 THOUSAND

2.0 UN Aid

The United Nations include in its Charter the aim "to achieve international co-operation in solving international problems of an economic, social, cultural or humanitarian character". Thus the UN member states are to endeavour the promotion of "higher standards of living, full employment, and conditions of economic and social progress and development". Still, states' aid contributions to multilateral agencies are a rather small percentage.

2.1 Multilateral approach for aid

Clearly, the advantages for donor countries to turn to international agencies with regard to foreign aid are[19]:

- The avoidance of "competitive intervention by rival nations"
- "U.N. action is taken in the name of the world community"
- "It is clearly in the interests of peace"
- "Its motivation is beyond suspicion or national or commercial ambition"
- "In some of the politically sensitive countries an international agency can lay down stricter conditions for aid than a single country"
- They are able to "draw on a world-wide pool of technical personnel"
- "internationally sponsored technical assistance can often be purchased at lower cost"

---

[19] Malek M.H., op.cit., pp. 215, 217-219

- They are "better equipped to help in regional projects overlapping national boundaries"
- They are "endowed with capacity to act in the interest of security and development", and "can promote the open world society of independent and prosperous nation"

With regard to Germany, the conducting of multilateral aid programmes is underlined according to these arguments[20]:

- stricter application of development policy criteria in the allocation of funds
- higher real value for the recipients since there are practically no price increase effects through aid-tying
- individual bilateral donors' foreign policy interests and the tendency towards prestige projects can be more easily kept in check
- greater participatory rights in the decision-making of international bodies
- savings in the administrative costs of smaller donor countries

On the other side, the counter-arguments against multilateral agencies and aid administration are[21]:

- lack of efficiency owing to the higher costs of large-scale administrative apparatus, and lengthy decision-making processes
- little potential for controlling international organizations
- little scope for presenting achievements to the donor country's public - with implications for parliamentary willingness to appropriate further funds

2.2 Germany and the UN

According to Tono Eitel, a retired senior diplomat, "in the course of the last 50 years, Germany has successfully risen from this pariah status to become a respected and full member of the UN."[22] Under the division of Germany and given the importance of acquiring international recognition during the Cold War, membership to the UN could only be successful for one of the states because of the veto of either the USA or the USSR. By 1973, both the GDR (Germany Democratic Republic) and the FRG (Federal Republic of Germany) were given 'inferior status' at the UN. Since then, involvement in the UN has been an essential part of Ger-

---

[20] ibid., p.60
[21] ibid., p.60
[22] http://www.german-embassy.org.uk/germany_at_the_un.html

many's foreign policy, being "a major cornerstone of the nation's peace, security and human rights policy"[23].

It was not until the reunification of Germany that full UN membership was eventually acquired. Since then, Gemany's contributions to the UN have been:

- a host country for UN secretariats and offices in Bonn (e.g. United Nations Volunteers programme, United Nations Information Centre, UN Convention to Combat Desertification);

- a member of the UN Security Council in 1977-8 / 1987-8 / 1995-6 / 2003-4;

- the presence of some Germans as UN staff and personnel for peace missions;

- the third largest contributor with 9% of UN annual budget; the "initiatives and statements of opinion in UN bodies" (e.g. in 1996, efforts in the Security Council to ban anti-personnel mines);

- member of the UN Human Rights Commission;

- chairmanship of the Iraq sanctions committee during the last membership of the Security Council. However, according to T. Eitel, "the permanent seat on the Security Council that Germany has occasionally eyed since the beginning of the 1990s will scarcely be able to count on American support in the foreseeable future".

With regard to financial contributions, in 2003 Germany committed 265 million euro {with 90 million euro as an assessed contribution, and 175 million euro being shared between specialized agencies and programmes such as the World Food Programme (WFP, 23 million euro), the United Nations Development Programme (UNDP, 25.7 million euro), the World Health Organization (WHO, 27 million euro) and the United Nations Environment Programme (UNEP, 8.2 million euro)} in UN development cooperation and about 435 million euro to the World Bank Group.[24]

Moreover, another important aspect of Germany's role in the United Nations is the fact that Germany is also the "third-largest shareholder in the World Bank after the US and Japan", and is therefore its own Executive Director. Germany hence enjoys some significant influence in the decision-making process and according to V. Meja, "the German government policy at the World Bank is an integral part of its development policy", which mainly focus on the aim of poverty eradication.[25] Indeed, with the challenges to be faced in this 21st century, i.e. the "ever more overwhelming number of people in need" with "more than a billion

---

[23] http://www.auswaertiges-amt.de/www/en/aussenpolitik/vn/vereinte_nationen/sitzstaat/sitz-dtl_html

[24] http://www.auswaertiges-amt.de/www/en/aussenpolitik/aussenwirtschaft/entwicklung/ez-vn_beteiligung_html

[25] http://www.afrodad.org/index.php?option=com_content&task=view&id=74&Itemid=38

people have to live on less than one US dollar per day", the economic crises, natural disasters and civil wars" which may "further exacerbate the social and humanitarian situation", require a multilateral approach, i.e. multilateral development cooperation for their tackling[26].

2.3 UN Millenium Development Goals (MDGs)

The MDGs made in 2000 and targeting their implementation by 2015, remain the context for dealing with the wide gap between the North and the South. These are[27]:

1. Eradicate extreme poverty and hunger
2. Achieve universal primary education
3. Promote gender equality and empower women
4. Reduce child mortality
5. Improve maternal health
6. Combat HIV/AIDS, malaria and other diseases
7. Ensure environmental sustainability
8. Develop a global partnership for development

2.4 Germany's 10-point Action Programme

To this effect, Germany's commitment is mainly centered on poverty alleviation and as such, a ten-point action programme has been drawn by the government and includes[28]:

- Boosting the economy and enhancing the active participation of the poor
- Realising the right to food and implementing agrarian reform
- Creating fair trade opportunities for the developing countries
- Reducing debt and financing development
- Guaranteeing basic social services and strengthening social protection
- Ensuring access to vital resources and fostering an intact environment
- Realising human rights and respecting core labour standards
- Fostering gender equality
- Ensuring the participation of the poor in social, political and economic life, and strengthening good governance
- Resolving conflict peacefully, and fostering human security and disarmament

---

[26] http://www.auswaertiges-amt.de/www/en/aussenpolitik/aussenwirtschaft/entwicklung/ez-vn_beteiligung_html
[27] http://www.un.org/millenniumgoals/
[28] http://www.bmz.de/en/service/glossary/aktionsprogramm2015.html
Program of Action 2015

Conclusion

According to its aid policy, development cooperation is perceived by Germany as a win-win policy since "combating hunger and poverty, bettering health standards and respecting human rights are prerequisites for the prevention of military conflicts – one of the greatest barriers to economic and social development in poor countries. Development cooperation thus helps maintain peace and security all over the world." Moreover, the Ifo Institute of Economic Research in its study in1999 found out that "one billion euro of development aid triggers long-term export growth of up to three billion euro and generates an increase of GDP of up to ten billion euro".[29]

Still, with regard to the UN, I tend to agree with S. Mansoob Murshed that,

> "whether or not the granting of aid is motivated by foreign policy considerations or a concern for common humanity, there are worries about the optimal pursuit of the chosen policies by those tasked to carry them out. In many instances, it might be better to delegate the authority for carrying out aid policy management to international organization rather than depend on national bodies. This certainly strengthens the case for a common pool approach to the funding of and access to development assistance. When aid is drawn from a common pool administered by an international agency, both policy ownership in developing countries and the transparency of the actual purpose of development assistance are strengthened."[30]

---

[29] <http://www.auswaertiges-amt.de/www/en/aussenpolitik/aussenwirtschaft/entwicklung/ez-vn_beteiligung_html>
German involvement in United Nations development cooperation
[30] S. Mansoob Murshed, Strategic interaction, Aid effectiveness and the formation of aid policies in donor nations, p.202

Annexes

MAIN INTERNATIONAL ORGANISATIONS, as of 15 June 2005
OFFICIAL CONTRIBUTIONS TO WHICH MAY BE REPORTED IN WHOLE OR IN PART AS ODA
Only contributions to organisations listed below are reportable as multilateral ODA or OA. Members should consult the Secretariat if they consider any developmental agencies are missing from this list.

1. UN Agencies, Funds and Commissions

- CCD Convention to Combat Desertification
- DLCO-EA Desert Locust Control Organisation for Eastern Africa
- ECA Economic Commission for Africa
- ECLA Economic Commission for Latin America
- ECWA Economic Commission for Western Asia
- ESCAP Economic and Social Commission for Asia and the Pacific
- IAEA International Atomic Energy Agency (voluntary contributions only)
- IFAD International Fund for Agricultural Development
- INSTRAW International Research and Training Institute for the Advancement of Women
- UNAIDS UN Programme on HIV/AIDS
- UNCDF United Nations Capital Development Fund
- UNCTAD United Nations Conference on Trade and Development
- UNDHA United Nations Department of Humanitarian Affairs
- UNDP United Nations Development Programme
- UNDRO United Nations Office of the Disaster Relief Co-ordinator
- UNEP United Nations Environment Programme
- UNETPSA United Nations Educational and Training Programme for Southern Africa
- UNFCC United Nations Framework Convention on Climate Change
- UNFPA United Nations Population Fund
- UN Habitat United Nations Human Settlement Programme
- UNHCR United Nations Office of the United Nations High Commissioner for Refugees
- UNICEF United Nations Children's Fund
- UNIDO United Nations Industrial Development Organisation
- UNIFEM United Nations Development Fund for Women
- UNITAR United Nations Institute for Training and Research
- UNMAS United Nations Mine Action Service
- UNOCHA United Nations Office of Co-ordination of Humanitarian Affairs
- UNODC United Nations Office on Drugs and Crime
- UNRISD United Nations Research Institute for Social Development
- UNRWA United Nations Relief and Works Agency
- UNSC United Nations System Staff College
- UNSCN United Nations System Standing Committee on Nutrition

- UNSIA United Nations Special Initiative on Africa
- UNU United Nations University (including Endowment Fund)
- UNV United Nations Volunteers
- UNVFD United Nations Voluntary Fund on Disability

- UNVFTC United Nations Voluntary Fund for Technical Co-operation in the Field of Human Rights
- UNVFVT United Nations Voluntary Fund for Victims of Torture
- WFC World Food Council
- WFP World Food Programme
- WPC World Population Conference

2. Other UN Contributions Reportable in Part

- FAO 51% Food and Agricultural Organisation
- ILO 15% International Labour Organisation
- ITU 18% International Telecommunications Union
- UNESCO 25% United Nations Educational, Scientific and Cultural Organisation
- UNO 12% United Nations Organisation

- UPU 16% Universal Postal Union
- WHO 70% World Health Organisation
- WIPO 3% World Intellectual Property Organisation
- WMO 4% World Meteorological Organisation

GERMANY

Net ODA	2003	2004	Change 2003/04
Current (USD m)	6 784	7 534	11.1%
Constant (2003 USD m)	6 784	6 788	0.1%
In Euro (million)	6 005	6 064	1.0%
ODA/GNI	0.28%	0.28%	
Bilateral share	60%	51%	
Net Official Aid (OA)			
Current (USD m)	1 181	1 434	21.5%

Top Ten Recipients of gross ODA/OA (USD million)	
1 China	396
2 Congo, Dem. Rep.	314
3 Nicaragua	307
4 Cameroon	278
5 Indonesia	163
6 India	157
7 Zambia	135
8 Egypt	134
9 Serbia & Montenegro	119
10 Turkey	104

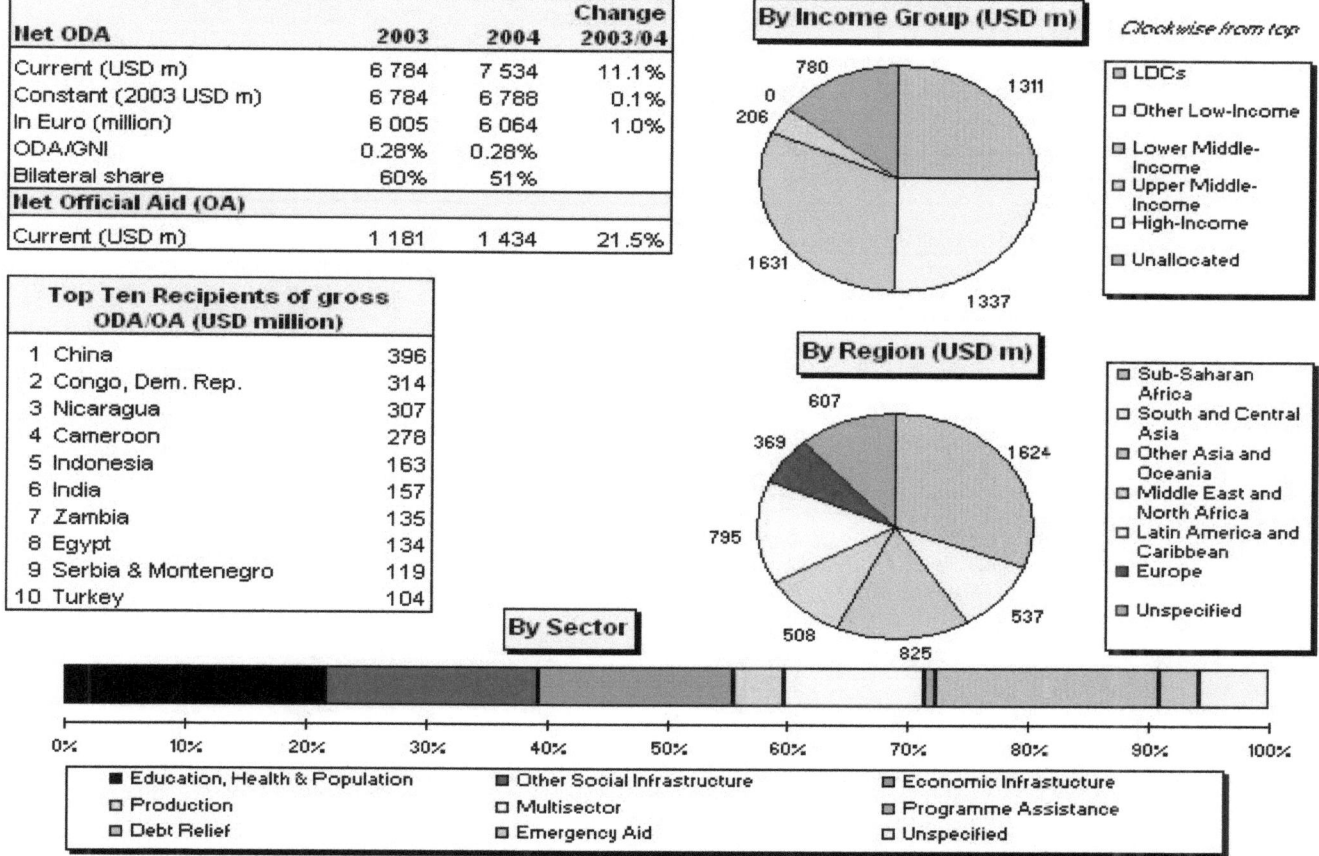

Source: OECD, DAC.
http://www.oecd.org/dac

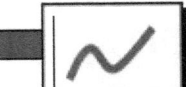

Net multilateral ODA flows to multilateral institutions and EU

€ million

Type of flow	1999	2000	2001	2002	2003
1. Grants or contributions to UN organisations and funds	**304,7**	**419,8**	**514,6**	**436,8**	**265,0**
- United Nations Development Programme (UNDP)	43,5	21,7	24,0	25,1	25,7
- United Nations Population Fund (UNFPA)	21,5	11,2	14,3	14,7	14,3
- United Nations Children's Fund (UNICEF)	5,5	4,4	4,4	5,1	5,1
- UN Relief and Works Agency for Palestine Refugees (UNRWA)	5,1	4,7	4,8	6,3	6,2
- United Nations High Commissioner for Refugees (UNHCR)	4,6	5,6	6,9	7,1	5,1
- World Food Programme (WFP)	23,0	23,0	23,0	23,0	23,0
- Food and Agriculture Organization (FAO)	15,3	18,2	18,4	26,0	23,1
- World Health Organisation (WHO)	29,4	35,0	37,3	33,4	27,0
- UN Educational, Scientific and Cultural Organization (UNESCO)	9,6	10,4	10,4	10,3	1,7
- United Nations Environment Programme (UNEP)	4,9	7,1	6,8	8,0	8,2
- United Nations Industrial Development Organization (UNIDO)	7,7	8,7	9,3	8,4	9,0
- other UN organisations	41,5	26,6	28,7	34,3	26,9
- other UN organisations (repayments)	-	-	-	-15,7	
- tied?? contributions to UN organisations	93,2	243,2	327,3	250',7	89',7
2. Grants for special purposes	**26,9**	**31,9**	**18,7**	**29,6**	**31,2**
- International agricultural research	17,9	14,3	14,3	14,3	15,0
- Other	9,0	17,5	4,4	15,3	16,2
3. Capital and fund subscriptions	**532,7**	**749,2**	**576,6**	**322,4**	**700,6**
a) World Bank Group	390,9	416,4	419,7	23,7	434,6
- World Bank (IBRD)	-	-	-	-	-
- International Development Association (IDA)	390,9	416,4	419,7	-	434,6
- International Finance Corporation (IFC)	-	-	-	-	
- MIGA	-	-			
b) Regional development banks	90,4	226,5	87,9	211,2	129,3
- Asian Development Bank (AsDB) and -Asian Development Fund (AsDF)	71,2	29,1	3,7	114,9	40,8
- African Development Bank (AfDB) and - African Development Fund (AfDF)	3,1	180,7	83,2	95,5	87,8
- Inter-American Development Bank (IDB), - Inter-American Fund for Special Operations (FSO) and - Inter-American Investment Corporation (IIC)	14,0	16,7	1,0	0,9	0,7
- Caribbean Development Bank (CDB) and - Caribbean Special Development Fund (SDF)	2,1	-	-	-	
c) Other institutions	51,5	106,3	69,1	87,5	136,7
- International Fund for Agricultural Development (IFAD)	-	9,9	8,6	10,1	
- Poverty Reduction and Growth Facility (PRGF-HIPC)	7,7	6,3	7,7	4,1	15,0
- LDC Fund					
- GEF and Montreal Protocol	43,8	90,1	52,8	73,3	116,7
- Rain Forest Trust Fund (RTF)					5,0
4. Contributions to the European Union	**1.236,0**	**1.342,0**	**1.275,3**	**1.329,7**	**1.414,5**
- European Development Fund (EDF)	486,2	468,3	296,0	379,7	513,9
- aid financed from the EU budget	756,5	879,9	985,2	956,0	905,4
- loans to the European Investment Bank (EIB)	-6,7	-6,2	-6,0	-6,0	-4,8
Total	**2.100,3**	**2.542,8**	**2.385,2**	**2.118,6**	**2.411,3**

Net multilateral ODA flows to multilateral institutions and EU

€ million

Type of flow	1999	2000	2001	2002	2003
1. Grants or contributions to UN organisations and funds	**304,7**	**419,8**	**514,6**	**436,8**	**265,0**
- United Nations Development Programme (UNDP)	43,5	21,7	24,0	25,1	25,7
- United Nations Population Fund (UNFPA)	21,5	11,2	14,3	14,7	14,3
- United Nations Children's Fund (UNICEF)	5,5	4,4	4,4	5,1	5,1
- UN Relief and Works Agency for Palestine Refugees (UNRWA)	5,1	4,7	4,8	6,3	6,2
- United Nations High Commissioner for Refugees (UNHCR)	4,6	5,6	5,9	7,1	5,1
- World Food Programme (WFP)	23,0	23,0	23,0	23,0	23,0
- Food and Agriculture Organization (FAO)	15,3	18,2	18,4	26,0	23,1
- World Health Organisation (WHO)	29,4	35,0	37,3	33,4	27,0
- UN Educational, Scientific and Cultural Organization (UNESCO)	9,6	10,4	10,4	10,3	1,7
- United Nations Environment Programme (UNEP)	4,9	7,1	6,8	8,0	8,2
- United Nations Industrial Development Organization (UNIDO)	7,7	8,7	9,3	8,4	9,0
- other UN organisations	41,5	26,6	28,7	34,3	26,9
- other UN organisations (repayments)	-	-	-	-15,7	
- tied?? contributions to UN organisations	93,2	243,2	327,3	250',7	89',7
2. Grants for special purposes	**26,9**	**31,9**	**18,7**	**29,6**	**31,2**
- International agricultural research	17,9	14,3	14,3	14,3	15,0
- Other	9,0	17,5	4,4	15,3	16,2
3. Capital and fund subscriptions	**532,7**	**749,2**	**576,6**	**322,4**	**700,6**
a) World Bank Group	390,9	416,4	419,7	23,7	434,6
- World Bank (IBRD)	-	-	-	-	-
- International Development Association (IDA)	390,9	416,4	419,7	-	434,6
- International Finance Corporation (IFC)	-	-	-	-	
- MIGA	-	-			
b) Regional development banks	90,4	226,5	87,9	211,2	129,3
- Asian Development Bank (AsDB) and					
-Asian Development Fund (AsDF)	71,2	29,1	3,7	114,9	40,8
- African Development Bank (AfDB) and					
- African Development Fund (AfDF)	3,1	180,7	83,2	95,5	87,8
- Inter-American Development Bank (IDB),					
- Inter-American Fund for Special Operations (FSO) and					
- Inter-American Investment Corporation (IIC)	14,0	16,7	1,0	0,9	0,7
- Caribbean Development Bank (CDB) and					
- Caribbean Special Development Fund (SDF)	2,1	-	-	-	
c) Other institutions	51,5	106,3	69,1	87,5	136,7
- International Fund for Agricultural Development (IFAD)	-	9,9	8,6	10,1	
- Poverty Reduction and Growth Facility (PRGF-HIPC)	7,7	6,3	7,7	4,1	15,0
- LDC Fund					
- GEF and Montreal Protocol	43,8	90,1	52,8	73,3	116,7
- Rain Forest Trust Fund (RTF)					5,0
4. Contributions to the European Union	**1.236,0**	**1.342,0**	**1.275,3**	**1.329,7**	**1.414,5**
- European Development Fund (EDF)	486,2	468,3	296,0	379,7	513,9
- aid financed from the EU budget	756,5	879,9	985,2	956,0	905,4
- loans to the European Investment Bank (EIB)	-6,7	-6,2	-6,0	-6,0	-4,8
Total	**2.100,3**	**2.542,8**	**2.385,2**	**2.118,6**	**2.411,3**

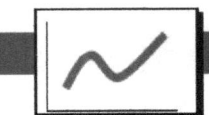

Bilateral ODA commitments by sector

Sector	2002		2003	
	€ million	%	€ million	%
Social infrastructure and services	**1.634,195**	**33,5**	**1.914,732**	**38,3**
Education	734,612	15,1	869,448	17,4
of which: basic education	77,227	1,6	76,557	1,5
Health	161,134	3,3	125,741	2,5
of which: basic health	84,507	1,7	54,780	1,1
Population policy/programmes and reproductive health	55,424	1,1	78,362	1,6
Water supply and sanitation, waste disposal	232,116	4,8	337,888	6,8
State and civil society	246,696	5,1	316,624	6,3
Other aspects of social infrastructure and services	204,213	4,2	186,670	3,7
Economic infrastructure and services	**540,744**	**11,1**	**597,291**	**11,9**
Transport and storage	190,276	3,9	162,719	3,3
Communications	19,765	0,4	5,130	0,1
Power generation and supply	114,615	2,3	180,867	3,6
Finance	147,985	3,0	161,245	3,2
Private business and other services	68,103	1,4	87,331	1,7
Productive sectors	**227,350**	**4,7**	**198,240**	**4,0**
Agriculture, forestry and fisheries	180,516	3,7	134,013	2,7
Industry, minerals and mining, construction	18,881	0,4	53,404	1,1
Trade and tourism	27,953	0,6	10,823	0,2
Multisector / cross-cutting	**527,474**	**10,8**	**580,430**	**11,6**
General environmental protection	88,422	1,8	92,947	1,9
Women and development	11,899	0,2	6,493	0,1
Other multisector measures	427,154	8,8	480,989	9,6
Commodity aid and general programme aid	**40,094**	**0,8**	**45,045**	**0,9**
Structural adjustment assistance together with World Bank/IMF	7,669	0,2	4,000	0,1
Food aid / food security	21,335	0,4	27,677	0,6
Other general programme and commodity aid	11,089	0,2	13,367	0,3
Debt relief	**1.304,086**	**26,7**	**1.214,575**	**24,3**
Emergency aid	**233,400**	**4,8**	**152,218**	**3,0**
Other	**370,230**	**7,6**	**295,932**	**5,9**
Administrative costs	259,669	5,3	220,061	4,4
Support for NGOs	3,885	0,1	1,083	0,0
Non-attributable measures	106,676	2,2	74,787	1,5
Total	**4.877,573**	**100,0**	**4.998,463**	**100,0**
for information:				
measures to fight AIDS	79,407	1,6	86,774	1,7

37-BilateraleODA-ZusagennachFrderbereichen2003-en 03.12.2004

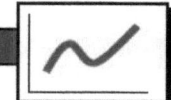

Total flows to developing countries

€ million

Type of flow	1998	1999	2000	2001	2002	2003
I. Official Development Assistance (ODA)	5.020,2	5.176,6	5.458,1	5.571,3	5.649,8	6.004,7
1. Bilateral	3.140,0	3.076,3	2.915,3	3.186,1	3.531,2	3.593,3
Grants	2.982,0	3.036,8	2.925,7	3.191,5	4.142,3	4.193,1
-- technical cooperation	1.788,0	1.793,9	1.779,1	1.773,5	1.889,8	2.035,3
-- other grants	1.194,0	1.242,9	1.146,6	1.418,0	2.252,5	2.157,8
Lending / other capital	158,0	39,4	-10,4	-5,3	-611,1	-599,8
2. European Union (EDF, EIB, EU budget)	1.104,3	1.236,0	1.342,0	1.275,3	1.329,7	1.414,6
3. Multilateral	775,9	864,3	1.200,9	1.109,9	788,8	996,8
Grants and capital subscriptions	777,1	865,6	1.203,8	1.113,3	792,2	1.000,9
-- United Nations	306,2	304,7	419,8	514,6	436,8	265,1
-- World Bank Group	306,5	390,8	416,4	419,7	23,7	434,6
-- regional development banks	99,5	90,3	226,5	87,9	211,2	129,4
-- other	64,8	79,7	141,1	91,1	120,5	171,8
Lending	-1,1	-1,3	-2,9	-3,3	-3,4	-4,1
II.Other Official Flows (OOF)	-289,1	-168,2	-494,7	-740,0	3.936,6	-3.154,3
1. Bilateral	-33,4	-40,3	-494,7	-740,0	3.936,6	-3.154,3
Export credits	268,0	334,7	-135,3	-172,1	-314,0	-392,6
Debt relief	-410,1	-473,5	-418,4	-530,4	4.170,8	-2.937,0
Other flows	108,6	98,5	59,0	-37,5	79,8	175,3
2. Multilateral	-255,6	-127,8	-	-	-	-
III. Private flows at market terms	14.577,2	12.838,1	7.499,1	1.351,0	-2.812,3	-459,5
1. Bilateral	13.383,6	13.070,2	9.309,8	2.319,4	-2.071,5	-47,5
Direct investment	5.146,7	5.282,8	4.869,6	2.081,7	343,4	1.094,5
Export credits	1.819,5	1.095,0	1.756,0	671,6	311,9	391,5
Other movements (portfolio/capital investments, lending)	6.417,4	6.692,4	2.684,2	-433,9	-2.726,8	-1.533,5
2. Multilateral	1.193,6	-232,1	-1.810,7	-968,4	-740,8	-412,0
IV. Private development cooperation	874,3	930,9	917,7	902,7	873,7	892,4
Total net disbursements	20.182,5	18.777,4	13.380,3	7.084,9	7.647,7	3.283,2
ODA as % of GNI [1]	0,26	0,26	0,27	0,27	0,27	0,28
Total flows as % of GNI	1,05	0,96	0,66	0,34	0,36	0,16
GNI (€ billion)	1.915,4	1.965,1	2.020,3	2.065,6	2.108,8	2.118,2

Footnotes:

[1] Gross National Income (Gross National Product)

21-GesamtleistungenanEntwicklungslnder2003-en 20.11.2004

Total flows to developing countries

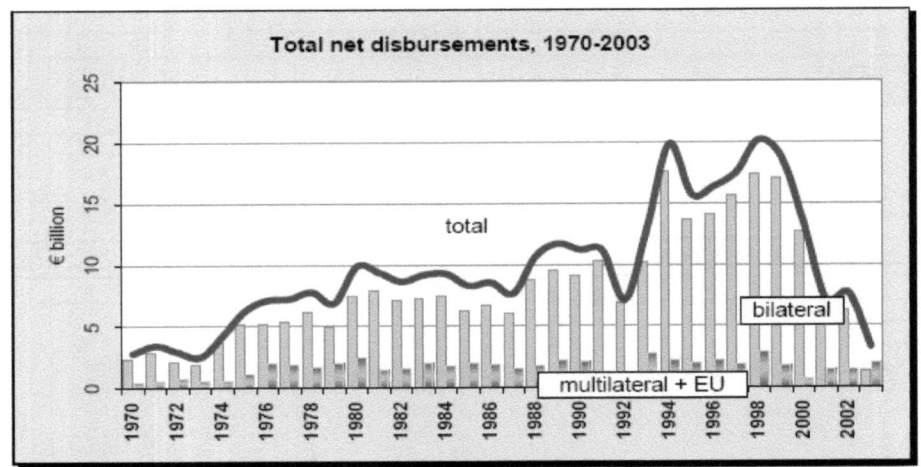

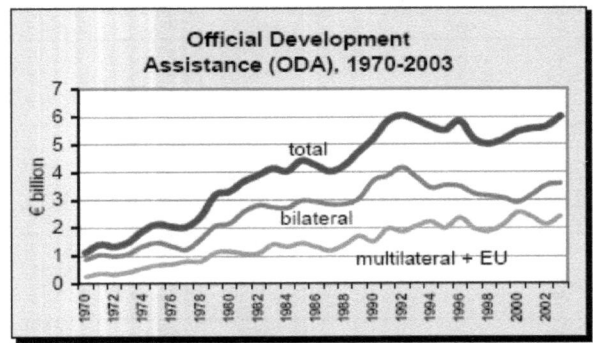

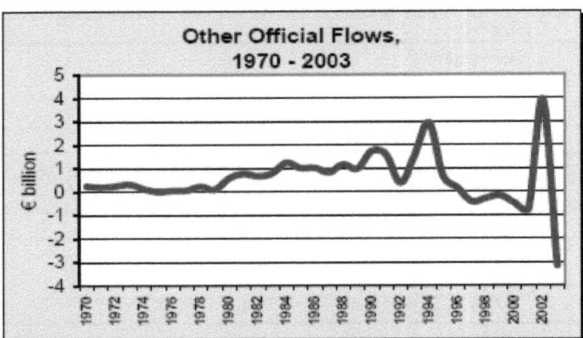

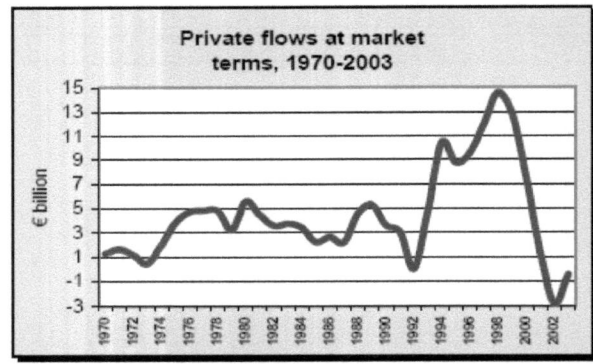

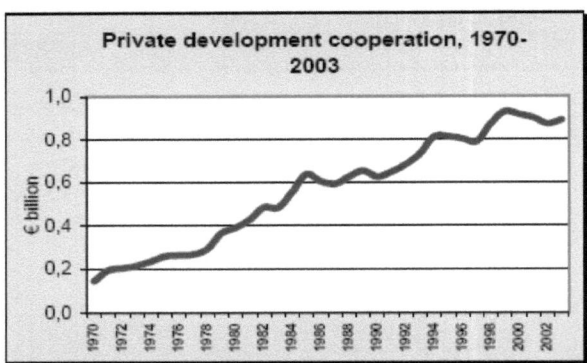

Total flows to developing countries

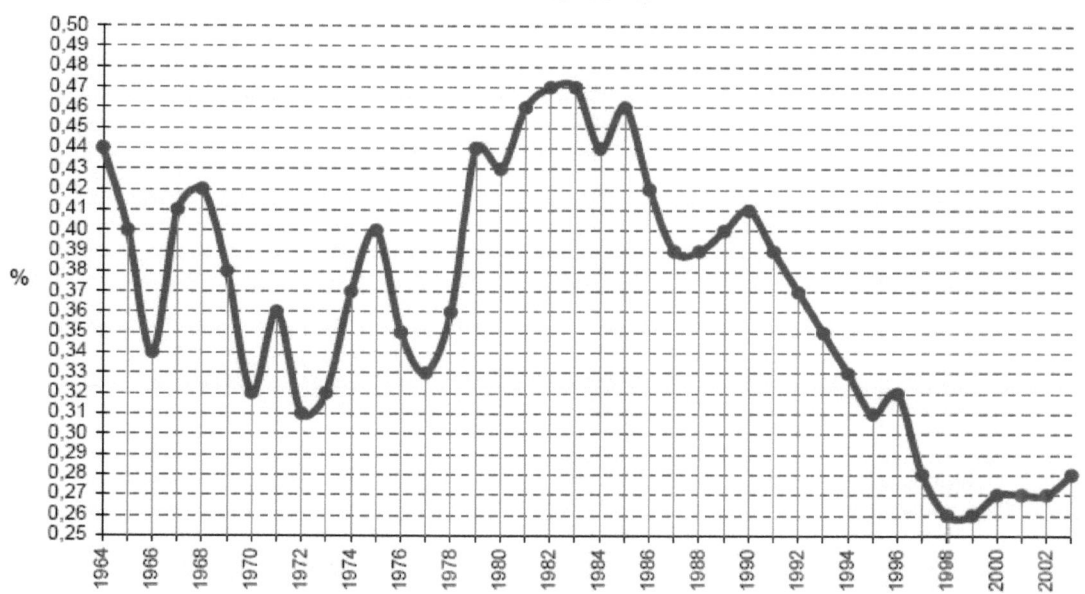

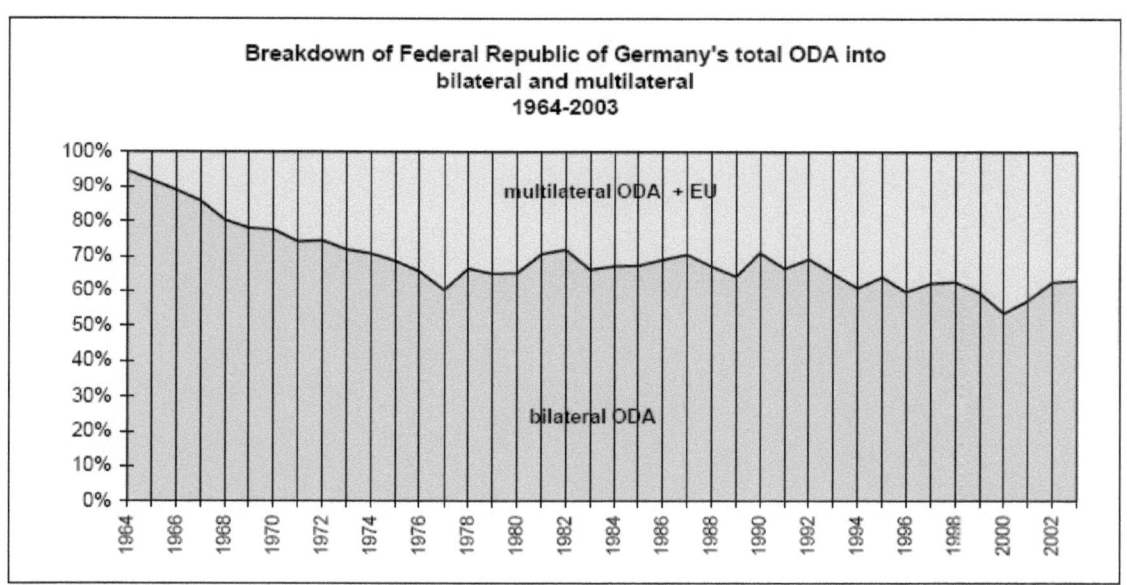

Comparison of donors - change since 2003 [1]

US$ million

	2003		2004 [3]		Change	
	ODA	ODA/GNI 2) %	ODA	ODA/GNI 2) %	absolute	relative
Australia	1.219	0,25	1.465	0,25	246	20,18%
Austria	505	0,20	691	0,24	186	36,83%
Belgium	1.853	0,60	1.452	0,41	-401	-21,64%
Canada	2.031	0,24	2.537	0,26	506	24,91%
Denmark	1.748	0,84	2.025	0,84	277	15,85%
Finland	558	0,35	655	0,35	97	17,38%
France	7.253	0,41	8.475	0,42	1.222	16,85%
Germany	6.784	0,28	7.497	0,28	713	10,51%
Greece	362	0,21	464	0,23	102	28,18%
Ireland	504	0,39	586	0,39	82	16,27%
Italy	2.433	0,17	2.484	0,15	51	2,10%
Japan	8.880	0,20	8.859	0,19	-21	-0,24%
Luxembourg	194	0,81	241	0,85	47	24,23%
Netherlands	3.981	0,80	4.235	0,74	254	6,38%
New Zealand	165	0,23	210	0,23	45	27,27%
Norway	2.042	0,92	2.200	0,87	158	7,74%
Portugal	320	0,22	1.028	0,63	708	221,25%
Spain	1.961	0,23	2.547	0,26	586	29,88%
Sweden	2.400	0,79	2.704	0,77	304	12,67%
Switzerland	1.299	0,39	1.376	0,37	77	5,93%
United Kingdom	6.282	0,34	7.836	0,36	1.554	24,74%
USA	16.254	0,15	18.999	0,16	2.745	16,89%
Total DAC	69.028	0,25	78.565	0,25	9.537	13,82%

[1] Taking account of both inflation and exchange rate movements

[2] Gross National Income (Gross National Product)

[3] provisional figures

Source: OECD / DAC

02-oda-gebervergleich-mit-2003-en.xls 31.10.2005

20

References:

📖 Malek M.H., Contemporary issues in European development aid, Avebury, Great Britain, 1991.

📖 May R. S. et al., Overseas aid - the impact on Britain and Germany, Harvester Wheatsheaf, Great Britain, 1989.

📖 Selim H., Development assistance policies and the performance of aid agencies, Macmillan Press, Hong Kong, 1983.

📖 White J., The politics of foreign aid, The Bodley Head, Great Britain,1974.

📖 Perroy H., L'Europe dans le tiers-monde, 1971.

📖 Kirdar, U., The structure of UN economic aid to underdeveloped countries, 1966.

📖 Clifford J. M. & Little I.M.D, International aid, George Allen and Unwin Ltd, Great Britain,1965.

📖 Feis H., Foreign aid and foreign policy, Macmillan, Great Britain, 1964.

➤ Mansoob Murshed S. "Strategic interaction, aid effectiveness and the formation of aid policies in donor nations", in *Journal of Economic Development*, Vol.28, No.1, June 2003, pp.189-203.

Retrieved in March 2006:

✍ <http://www.german-embassy.org.uk/germany_at_the_un.html>
Tono Eitel, *Foreign and Security Policy Germany in the United Nations.*

✍ <http://www.auswaertiges-amt.de/www/en/aussenpolitik/aussenwirtschaft/entwicklung/ez-vn_beteiligung_html>
German involvement in United Nations development cooperation (last updated in September 2005)

✍ <http://www.bmz.de/en/principles/index.html>
Reducing poverty, building peace, promoting equitable forms of globalisation.

✍ <http://www.bmz.de/en/service/glossary/aktionsprogramm2015.html>
Program of Action 2015.

✍ <http://www.bmz.de/en/figures/GermanContribution/index.html>
The BMZ's budget is on the increase.

✍ http://www.tatsachen-ueber-deustchland.de/645.0.html
Federal foreign office: United Nations.

✍ <http://www.auswaertiges-amt.de/www/en/aussenpolitik/vn/vereinte_nationen/sitzstaat/sitz-dtl_html
Germany as a United Nations host country.

✍ http://www.afrodad.org/index.php?option=com_content&task=view&id=74&Itemid=38
Vitalice Meja, *The Power of Shares in the World Bank – The Case of Germany*, in African Forum and Network on Debt and Development (AFRODAD Lobby and Advocacy)

✍ http://www.un.org/millenniumgoals/
UN Millennium Development Goals.